Keep Your Eyes On The PRIZE

AN EXERCISE IN LIFE PURPOSE, RANDOM ACTS OF KINDNESS AND GENEROSITY

Frederick Pearce and Angela Christensen

ISBN: 1-4196-9023-X
ISBN-13: 9781419690235

Visit www.booksurge.com to order additional copies.

CONTENTS

Preface.. 7

Discover Your Life Purpose.. 9

Random Acts of Kindness 63

Gratitude 83

Taking Action 107

Epilogue.. 115

ACKNOWLEDGEMENTS

Members of SuccessVibe and the Anthony Robbins internet discussion forum - Suzy, Joanne, Cat Lover, Paul, Greg, Mudd, and all the others. We thank them for their participation and their permission to use their thoughts and ideas.

Thanks to Tom for letting us explore the possibilities of this book on his website, and to Mark for his encouragement.

And thanks to Wanda Layton for her help in getting this book published.

* * *

PREFACE

Keep Your Eyes On The Prize is a collaboration between two budding writers who met on the internet. As this book goes to press, they have not met in person but pursue their individual search for excellence by helping each other reach their goals online - a true twenty-first century friendship.

Angela Christensen lives in Alberta, Canada, and has an extensive background in crime prevention and disaster relief. She also does voice-overs for commercials and documentaries. By working on her own issues, she came to learn about gratitude, random acts of kindness and living her spirituality, sharing it with everyone she meets.

Frederick Pearce is a business mentor and can claim a wide experience in business, with a career spanning forty-five years working for large multinationals, medium-sized local companies and small businesses of his own. He is well-traveled: starting from his birthplace of England, he has visited over thirty different countries from the Middle East to the United States, including living and working in seven of them. He is now retired - apart from a few speaking engagements - and lives in Texas.

Angela and Frederick met on an internet forum, where they discovered they had something to learn from one another's friendship. Frederick learned from Angela the gift of gratitude and offering random acts of kindness, things he had overlooked in his rushed, technical world. This created an inner peace that Frederick had lacked until then. Angela learned about the importance of discovering the purpose of her life by following thought provoking exercises Frederick showed her. Not only was this inspiring to Angela, it changed the course of her life. Discovering her life's purpose, she knew it was time to use her writing talents for the world at large, in the hopes of helping others. Angela continues to help others through her volunteer work as well.

We hope you enjoy reading and learning as much as we enjoyed writing and sharing.

Feel free to write in this book. You will find space provided for you to use this book as a Workbook. Or you can use a separate exercise book.

Have fun!

–Angela Christensen

–Frederick Pearce

* * *

Discover Your Life Purpose
by
Frederick Pearce

LIFE PURPOSE: AN INTRODUCTION

A very successful insurance salesman was asked, "What is the secret of your success?" He thought for a moment, then smiled and replied, "I have the uncanny ability to always miss a two foot putt!" It probably helps to be a golfer *and* a salesman to understand the irony.

I was thinking of that story in the shower this morning, and I started wondering about this thing called the "secret of success." People must have been wanting to be successful since before time was invented. Surely, by now all the success principles are well known, aren't they? What could possibly be a secret, anymore?

Napoleon Hill refers to a "secret" throughout his classic book, *"Think and Grow Rich,"* but he doesn't actually say what it is. When I asked a couple of friends what they thought this secret was, one friend replied, "The way one thinks is the 'master key' to what one gets in life." The other said, "Unstoppable determination. Hill gives a lot of stories to the effect of never giving up."

For me, the "secret" in *Think and Grow Rich* is "definiteness of purpose" – in other words, Life Purpose, or focus – whether one focuses on the whole life journey, or on individual projects. But these things are not secret - all three ingredients are known to be essential to success. There are other things, of course - gratitude and kindness, for example - and none of *them* are secret, either.

So, what's with this "secret" idea?

If people like Aristotle and Plato, Thomas Edison, Andrew Carnegie, John D. Rockefeller, Henry Ford, Marshall Field, and many, many others knew about some secret ingredient for success, wouldn't the world know it by now?

I think the point is that there is no such "secret."

All the ingredients for success are known. Anyone - everyone - YOU - can be more successful than you are. You have applied the ingredients of success only as much as it takes to get to the level you are at now. Albert Einstein is supposed to have said, "A problem cannot be solved at the level of thinking that caused it." The problem has to be approached from a higher level of thinking. To reach a higher level of thinking, you just have to apply the known ingredients more effectively or more diligently. It's not a matter of more knowledge; what is required is better thinking.

Claiming that there is something hidden - a secret - is to trick people into believing that the reason they aren't more successful is because some part of a puzzle has been denied them, hidden from them. This not only plays on envy, it evokes jealousy and a desire to gain what others are denied. Envy, jealousy and greed are very negative and dangerous emotions. These emotions are not conducive to success. So authors, screenwriters and speakers who employ this "I know the secret" concept are using it to entice others to buy their book, movie, or audio tapes - yet they don't necessarily contain anything beyond what is public knowledge and quite un-secret.

I have read Napoleon Hill, Dale Carnegie, Brian Tracy, Og Mandino and others, and many allude to a secret, but most never quite come out and say what it is. There are hints that it might be the Golden Rule – Do unto others as you would be done by. Perhaps it might be determination, willpower, purpose, or creating win-win situations. It can all be interpreted to mean whatever you think it means. They are all helpful books, certainly, but is this common reference to a secret nothing more than a marketing ploy?

Perhaps the whole "secret" thing is rather overplayed. I don't believe there is or ever was a conspiracy keeping "success secrets" secret. It just sounds too farfetched for me. Calling it a secret creates an excuse for not having succeeded in the past. Blaming one's own lack of success on a conspiracy doesn't seem credible. But if you are not honest with yourself, you'll have nothing but excuses anyway. If someone is not successful it is not because they don't know a particular secret, it's because they are simply not doing the things they should be doing to achieve their goals. They lack discipline or focus or follow-through or strategy. But they do not, generally, lack the knowledge.

I don't think Napoleon Hill was misusing this idea of a "secret" in *Think and Grow Rich*. He was probably using the "secret" dodge to get readers to concentrate more on the message and so learn the lessons better. He wasn't selling the secret as such, as others who came later have. His reference to a secret in *Think and Grow Rich* was primarily to make you curious and to make you think and to draw your own conclusions, which may be different for each reader. The danger with focussing on "a secret" is that you might too easily buy into the concept that this "secret" is the missing key that will finally give you success - that lack of success to date is not your fault, it's because you did not know "the secret." And then to suppose that this "secret" is the only thing you need to gain success. I think this is dangerous. It is searching for new knowledge because we have failed to master the existing knowledge.

To master existing knowledge, we must focus on and practice the fundamentals. But fundamentals aren't attractive or flashy, and many people look for new, exciting information and especially new "secrets" because they want success with less effort. As soon as I hear someone say, "Teach me something new!" I know that person is not into mastering the subject. Yet, applying the basics of a subject doesn't call for a great deal of effort, just steady, consistent application of known principles.

Success comes from within us, not from outside. We don't attract opportunity, we open our eyes to the opportunity that is all around us. It has always been there! Winston Churchill is often quoted as saying, "Every day, people stumble over opportunity but most just pick themselves up, brush themselves off, and hurry along as if nothing had happened."

To think that opportunity or money or love or anything else is going to remain absent in your life unless you discover "the secret" creates a separation between you and what you seek. It also creates a dependence on the seller of "the secret." If you recognize that all those things are always around you and all you have to do is notice them and reach out for them, then you become connected to them, naturally, with no dependencies.

Every definite purpose in life involves service to self and others. We all follow our Life Purpose in some way, whether we know it or not. If we are not clear on that purpose, the path can be difficult and erratic. If we know our Life Purpose, we can live it lightly and happily. It's a matter of personal discovery. Think, "What am I doing right now that fits a purpose in life for me? If exploring my passions helps me discover my purpose, how do I express my life passions right now in different aspects of my life?" Most express passions in several ways to different degrees: with words, with actions, with thought and emotion. Expanded thinking is a key to discovering a purpose in life.

Napoleon Hill talks of Life Purpose right from the first pages of his book; his first chapter is entitled "Thoughts Are Things," and the very first words of that first chapter are: "Truly, thoughts are things, and powerful things at that when they are mixed with definiteness of purpose...."

"Definiteness of purpose!"

You can't get stronger than that. A well-defined Life Purpose is the most important step on the road to success. Unfortunately, *Think and Grow Rich* does not have a section on *how* to develop a Life Purpose.

That is the gap this book is designed to fill.

—Frederick Pearce

LIFE PURPOSE

"I am the dance of a candle-flame. I play, illuminate, tease! My world is so amazingly abundant I sparkle like a child in a toyshop. Life is to explore and have fun with, and I delight in provoking others to do the same. Excellence is my Guiding Principle for excellence is the path to success however I choose to measure success. I take pride in achieving excellence: I enjoy attracting wealth. Yet, my happiness is not outside to be gathered in; it is inside, a product of my own vibrancy. I strive for elegance and eloquence, and always manage to be surprised by the results. I am a voyager: along the way I meet other travelers and add to their bounty however I can. By being faithful to my principles I earn respect and honor, but what I cherish most is the simple satisfaction of a job well done."

The above is my Life Purpose statement. I wrote it several years ago and refer to it constantly. I can't say it's taken me from poverty to power, because, although I started life in a low-income family, I have never been in a state of real poverty. I have been deeply in debt, though, and I can say the process of developing a Life Purpose statement changed my life.

I was a frustrated, often angry, hard-driving work-a-holic: I became happier, kinder, more productive, and much more relaxed and fulfilled. It has allowed me to keep looking towards the future. I know that the improvements in my life and gains in my material circumstances are a result of discovering my Life Purpose. The subsequent steps of creating a mission statement and personal motto enabled me to define and follow through on the changes I needed to make. I'm now better off than I could ever have imagined.

As I look back over the years, I can say that I've had a very good life. I'm grateful for that, now, but gratitude isn't something I spent much time over in the past. I developed a penchant for being good at my work and being right. My profession was quite adversarial, and that required me to be a perfectionist, too. I took it as something to be proud of when I was described, behind my back, as someone who had lots of enemies but they all wanted me on their side!

My work gave direction to my life even though it could be quite frustrating. My life had structure and order. When I moved away from this style of work, I began to drift. I soon began to long for the high-pressure worklife I had been living, knowing all the while that I would not be happy if I returned to it. I guess I was burned out!

I started to take an interest in self-improvement. I needed to do something – I was unhappy, my marriage was on thin ice because of my attitude, I was decidedly unproductive and my savings were diminishing. Ah! So this is what a mid-life crisis is, is it?

Someone started talking to me about setting goals – long-range, lifetime goals. I remember this person saying, "If you don't know where you are going, you won't know how to get there." And I remember thinking, "If I had known where I was going, I'd have missed all those strange and exciting 'ports-in-a-storm' I have experienced. I rather enjoyed them, thank you!"

Nevertheless, the drifting feeling persisted.

Later, someone else spoke to me in religious terms of having purpose in my life. I countered with, "No thank you to that, too. The whole beauty of life, in my view, is that it has no purpose. I don't want to be confined by a set of long-term goals. I want the wide-open space of freedom."

And, the drifting feeling persisted.

Then, later still, a friend hit the button: "Your life doesn't have to *have* purpose," they said, "You can give it purpose. And you can change that purpose any time you want."

"Hey! Now we're talking!"

At first, I just copied their Life Purpose statement and changed a few words to make it more relevant to what I wanted my life to be. Then something happened – my Life Purpose statement seemed to take on a life of its own. If it was going to be my Life Purpose statement, it had to be about *my* life. And because I had written what I wanted in the present tense as if I had these things already, I began to see that, in fact, I *did* have these things already.

For example, my perfectionism was a pursuit of excellence, so excellence was *always* my guiding principle. I had used elegance and eloquence in the form of aloofness and tough negotiation in my role as an adversary. Being already well-traveled visiting and living and working in so many different countries, I *was* a voyager. Being the best and being right all the time *did* provide the satisfaction of a job well done.

What I had been in the past was congruent with what I wanted out of life. My values and my life were one! And moving forward was a natural extension of where I had been. I suddenly realized that we cannot escape our true nature. If we do nothing about what we are, what we are will control our destiny. I believe it is within our power to change what we are, but if we make no effort to change it, what we are will direct our lives. Therefore, identifying your values and discovering your Life Purpose is the first, and most important, step in changing your life, and therefore changing your fortune.

Why bother? Why not just let life happen? Be yourself? Be true to yourself? Because our true nature is modified by circumstance and can take subtle and, sometimes, not very pleasant divergent paths. Perfectionism is not generally considered a virtue, but excellence is. Being right all the time is not considered a virtue, but doing a job to the best of your ability is.

As I studied my thesaurus to find exactly the right words, I began to realize that my Life Purpose statement was helping me identify the excesses – like perfectionism – so that I could control them and modify them to be a better, more likable person. While I was happy about being good at my job, I didn't like having so many enemies.

My combined Life Purpose statement, mission statement and personal motto, created for me:

— a realization of who I am, truly;

— clarity as to what tendencies have, and might continue to, lead me away from a fully satisfying life;

— identified my excesses;

— pointed out my virtues;

— provided a clear, unjumbled environment in which I can function as a human being;

— and has given me a framework to plan out practical steps towards my goals;

— while allowing maximum freedom to change, modify or momentarily set aside those goals, if I so choose.

For some people, having a Life Purpose is just another phrase. To me it is a way of life. It is my prime strategy for living an extraordinary life. And that, my friend, is The Prize.

Ok. Let's get started.

We are going to help you determine your values, discover your Life Purpose, create a Life Purpose statement, a mission statement and a personal motto.

Let's do it!

Do You Want to Live an Extraordinary Life?

I have heard it said that having a stated Life Purpose is restrictive. You might stick so rigidly to it that you miss opportunities along the way. I felt that for much of my life. But believing that is to misunderstand what a Life Purpose is.

A Life Purpose is not something you create – which could be restrictive. Your Life Purpose is what you are. You discover it.

Now you could be restricted by what you are, but it is what you are, and you would not be restricting yourself per se. For example, I am an energetic person. That's what I am – it's "who" I am. My ability to relax is thus restricted but I do not restrict myself as such. By recognizing this energy in myself, I can now make a conscious effort to relax, when appropriate, and so create what I might have missed. A Life Purpose is liberating, not restricting.

I often have my coaching clients create a Life Purpose statement for themselves because it does help them get their lives together and headed in the right direction. I have found mine very useful in focussing on what is important to me. This has created for me a wonderful sense of peace and control, even when surrounded by chaos.

The following exercise comprises discovering your Life Purpose, creating a Life Purpose statement, a mission statement and a personal motto.

The reason behind it is this: life is easier, more productive and more fulfilling when you are comfortable within yourself, and goals are more easily achieved if you reach them in the direction your life is already taking. It is rather like driving from Texas to New York in which a goal to visit California would take you away from your purpose, but a goal to visit

Virginia will take you closer to accomplishing your purpose.

The First Step – Your Most Important Values

You can learn a great deal about yourself and your business or career by asking questions about your values. Make a list of values. Here are some. You may think of others and can add them.

Gratitude... ...Freedom... ...Adventure.... ...Beauty... ...Love... ...Fulfillment... ...Growth... ...Excitement... ...Courage... ...Self-expression... ...Self-esteem... ...Learning... ...Health... ...Humor... ...Passion... ...Creativity... ...Kindness... ...Security... ...Honesty... ...Resourcefulness... ...Communication... ...Integrity... ...Power... ...Acceptance... ...Respect... ...Intelligence... ...Family connection... ...Spiritual connection... ...Emotional connection... ...Making a difference... ...Independence... ...Challenge... ...Being the best... ...Someone to share life with... ...Fun... ...Enjoyment... ...Recognition... ...Contribution...

...Others: (Write in)................ ....

....

....

1. Circle or highlight the values in the above list that are important to you and leave out those that are not so important. If you find you have circled many, go through them again and cross out the values that are less important.

2. Now choose the five most important values from your shortened list. Write your five most important values here—

1 ....

2 ....

3 ....

4 ....

5 ....

3. Your objective is to find five values that are so meaningful and important to you that they can complete the sentence:

Without [value], life would have no meaning.

Fill in the blanks with your most important values—

Without ...., life would have no meaning.

Without ...., life would have no meaning.

Without ...., life would have no meaning.

Without ...., life would have no meaning.

Without ...., life would have no meaning.

4. Now choose one of the five that is more important than any other.

....

And, repeat the test – Without ...., life would have no meaning. If this statement is not true, go back and find the value for which this statement *is* true.

5. This most important value has probably had more effect on your life to date than anything else! Together, the list of five values is a blueprint for your life.

What Value Values?

What are values? – morals? ethics? beliefs? priorities? I think your values are whatever you care about most. What you care about most could have ethical meaning, could have moral implications, might concern your beliefs and probably do constitute your priorities. But the deciding question surely must be, Do you value it? – and to me, the way to discover your most important values is to complete the statement....

Without (value) my life would be worthless.

Without freedom my life would be worthless.

Without love my life would not be worth living.

Without happiness I'd rather be dead.

....whatever it is for you.

It's possible to become confused trying to decide which values to list. So much is involved – your morals, your ethics, your goals, your desires. When I was trying to get my Life Purpose sorted out, I felt confused, too. Just keep at it. Eventually your most important values will reveal themselves. I found a good night's sleep helped.

I believe there is a definite path to follow. Of course, there are always many paths to a common destination and I'm not trying to say that my way is the only way, but I have found – for myself and when coaching others – that the simplest path is this—

1. Determine your most important values.
2. Reduce the list to the five most important values.
3. Pick the one value that is most important of all.
4. Use the five most important values to create a Life Purpose statement.
5. From that determine a mission statement.
6. From that determine a personal motto.

Many people try to write a mission statement before knowing what their Life Purpose is – this seems to me to be doing it backwards. Any attempt to write a mission statement before you have discovered your Life Purpose and most important values is going to create confusion and misdirection.

The Horse Goes in Front of the Cart!

Joanne said to me: "This is what I come up with when I think about my purpose in life:

'*My main purpose in life is to get my kids through their life, to make people laugh, to be loving, caring and a great listener, to help others.*' "

At this point, Joanne had not listed her five most important values. I told Joanne that I thought she was jumping the gun. My reasoning is this – to attempt to write your Life Purpose statement before you have identified your most important values will cause confusion and leave you unsettled about the future. Your Life Purpose statement needs the support of your most important values and, without that, may not even represent your Life Purpose at all.

First the values; second, the Life Purpose. You may come to the same result, but not necessarily, and you cannot know if your Life Purpose is in step with your most important values until you have determined what your most important values are. And if your Life Purpose statement and your values are not consistent with one another, you will have your values pulling you in one direction and your goals pulling you in a different direction. That is a recipe for a life of indecision and frustration.

Imagine reaching the end of your life, or the end of the period you set for achieving your goals; imagine achieving your goals and feeling disappointed — thinking, "Is this all there is?!"

Joanne did the values exercise and came back with her five most important values—

1. Family
2. Health
3. Love
4. Happiness
5. Security

She was now ready for the final part of Step #1, which is for her to satisfy herself that the five values she has listed truly are her most important values.

Can they each complete the sentence, Without ... (value) ..., my life would be worthless.

Without ...Family..., my life would be worthless.
Without ...Health..., my life would be worthless.
Without ...Love..., my life would be worthless.
Without ...Happiness..., my life would be worthless.
Without ...Security..., my life would be worthless.

Confirm to yourself, before moving on, that your #1 value truly is your absolutely single most important value, without which your life would not be worth living. If you are not sure, go back and do this part again until you are sure you have the values that are most important to you.

Did you notice, by the way, that your #1 value has had a particularly influential effect on your life so far? If it hasn't, it's probably not your most important value! Go back and do the values exercise again.

Only Five Values Needed

Many people have difficulty reducing their list of most important values down to five. While five is not a magic number, more than five can get clumsy, so make every effort to have no more than five to use for this exercise. You will obviously have more than five values, but only the most important five are needed for your Life Purpose statement.

A client (who wishes only to be identified as Cat Lover) was having difficulty deciding which were her five most important values. Eventually, she got it!

She said, "I feel good about what I have done with my 'homework'... I went inside, to that place of spirituality and gratitude – and worked on my values again."

This is what she came up with—

1. Contribution
2. Integrity
3. Courage
4. Expression
5. Growth

She previously had Vitality and Freedom on her list but dropped them. She asked herself, "Can I live without Vitality and Freedom in my life?" The answer was "yes" to those two items, so they had to go.

Cat Lover went on to explain: "I am reminded of Victor Frankl who wrote a book about being in a Nazi concentration camp... while he had no physical freedom, his spirit was still free. So I took freedom off my list." She took Freedom off her list because, like Victor Frankl, without freedom her life would not be worthless.

Then she explained about Vitality, and how she had included it because her friend was so vital and she wanted to be like that, too. That doesn't work, though.

Cat Lover: "My friend is so VITAL... she is like sunshine or air to us... hard to live without! I was trying to include more of her approach to life in my statement... but alas, it didn't feel like something I would say.... although I try to be vital... it doesn't resonate with me on a deeper level."

These are to be *your* values, not someone else's. Look over your five most important values again — Are they truly *your* values, or are they someone else's values?

The Life Purpose Statement

Cat Lover went ahead and wrote her Life Purpose statement—

"My purpose in being on this planet – is living in harmony with all, in glorious abundance and prosperity. I balance my courage and desire, and use all my skills, talents and abilities for the higher good of all. I demand the best of myself always. With faith and confidence I express myself openly – from my heart and soul. I step forward into the light of my highest self in all I chose to do and become. As I grow ever more grateful everyday, for all the abundance and blessings in my life. I enhance humanity in all I say and do."

She said it feels right! For who she is now, for who she wants to become, and for how she visualizes being in the future. But this identified a common problem, and it is set out here (with Cat Lover's permission) in case readers stumble into this difficulty, too.

There is no doubt this Life Purpose statement is very inspirational. Yet, I do not see Cat Lover's Life Purpose as being congruent with her stated values. She may, and that's what matters, but here are my observations, in case others find the same happening to them.

The first – and therefore most important – value stated in Cat Lover's Life Purpose is Harmony. That doesn't even appear in her list of most important values. Abundance and Prosperity are closely associated with Harmony – and they don't appear as most important values, either. Here is Cat Lover's Life Purpose statement again—

*"My purpose in being on this planet – is living in **harmony** with all, in glorious **abundance** and prosperity. I balance my **courage** and desire, and use all my skills, talents and abilities for the higher good of all. I demand the best of myself always. With **faith** and **confidence** I express myself openly – from my heart and soul. I step forward into the light of my highest self in all I chose to do and become. As I grow ever more grateful everyday, for all the **abundance** and **blessings** in my life. I enhance humanity in all I say and do."*

Courage is mentioned (#3 value) and a hint at Contribution (#1 value), in the second sentence.

The third sentence is about demanding the best of herself. This is not mentioned in any form I can see in her list of values.

Faith and Confidence – fourth sentence – not mentioned in her most important values. Gratitude, Abundance, again, and Blessings (more Abundance) are mentioned, and finishes with another hint only at Contribution.

It seems to me the stated most important values and the Life Purpose are not saying the same thing. You don't want to have a Life Purpose that does not support and is not supported by your most important values, because that will lead to profound incoherence in your life journey. Your values will pull you one way, your Life Purpose will pull you another.

Suppose you had a most important value of Family Connection and a Life Purpose statement that included a desire to travel and live and work in foreign countries. Could you have both? Imagine Safety, Comfort and Security were most important values for you and your

Life Purpose statement had you looking for excitement and adventure? Are you likely to follow your Life Purpose statement?

Can you see what I'm saying? Read Cat Lover's values and the Life Purpose again and see if you can see the disconnect.

Reader, what is happening with *your* Life Purpose statement? Have you found a disconnect between your values and your life statement? How would you rearrange things to make them congruent?

A Life Purpose that is So "Right!"

If your Life Purpose statement sounds so "right" once you have written it, but your most important values seem to have been overlooked, there are only two possibilities—

1. It could be that you have mistaken your most important values, or

2. Your Life Purpose is something you think you ought to do, or you have been thinking all along that's what you want, but it isn't!

Cat Lover's life statement sounds to me like it flows from a person with values like:

1. Abundance
2. Harmony
3. Being the best I can be
4. Courage
5. Gratitude

Instead of what she stated:

1. Contribution
2. Integrity
3. Courage
4. Expression
5. Growth

Compare Cat Lover's Life Purpose statement with the two different lists of most important values and see which list you think is more in tune.

Doing Step 2.

This is how I want you to do Step #2 in order to prevent the disconnect from happening. Use your most important values that you listed earlier to create the core of a Life Purpose statement. This isn't the Life Purpose statement yet, but is an intermediary step towards it.

Let's practice first by using an imaginary list of values. Using the values below...

Confidence, plus
Adventure,
Health,
Humor, and
Honesty

...one could arrive at a basic Life Purpose statement like this: – *"I am a confident person who loves adventure; I am grateful for my health and strive to maintain it; I see the humor in life and deal with life honestly, and expect others to be honest with me."*

Here's the format – I "am" (the first value) who "likes to" or who "does" (the other values)

Let's try another example:

Acceptance is the #1 value, followed by
Creativity,
Independence,
Self-expression and
Respect.

A basic Life Purpose statement based on the above values might be – *"I am gregarious and being accepted by others is fundamental to my being: I am creative with an independence that shows itself in self-expression; while I am respectful of others, I expect respect in return."*

Try this one yourself:

#1 Most important value : Security
Next most important value : Fulfillment
Next most important value : Integrity
Next most important value : Making a difference
Next most important value : Someone to share life with.

Starting with the #1 most important value, write a basic statement using the values mentioned above...

I am .... who ....

and.. and.............

....and..............................

....

After some soul-searching, here's what Cat Lover came up with for her original list of most important values of Contribution, Integrity, Courage, Expression and Growth—

"My Life Purpose is to be a published author, thereby helping people through contribution, writing with love and integrity, using my new found courage to continually be the best me I can be, expressing myself for the highest good of all – and continuing to grow and learn."

Isn't that better? Doesn't this Life Purpose express Cat Lover's most important values? By living her most important values, is she not now fulfilling her true Life Purpose? That's how to live an extraordinary life – a life in which your values and your actions are consistent with each other. And that is why a Life Purpose statement is a principal success strategy.

You may have noticed that Cat Lover included a little mission statement – to be a published author. This isn't needed in a Life Purpose statement. What if she had written: *"I am a giver who helps people by contributing with love and integrity, using my courage to be the best I can be, expressing myself for the highest good of all, and continuing to grow and learn."*

Now she is free to pursue her Life Purpose as a giver in other ways besides being a published author.

It is time for you to create your own Life Purpose statement, using your own most important values, starting with your #1 value first and the other four in any order. Just place your five most important values in a line and try to string them together in a single sentence. Keep it simple and basic for now. We will dress it up later.

First, list your five most important values again—

1......................... 2.......................... 3..........................

4....................... 5..........................

Now, string them together —

I "am" (the first value) who "likes to" (the other values.)

Do it now – fill in the blanks —

I am .... who likes to ....

.... and ....

and.. and ....

and I expect .... in return.

Notice the little addition at the end? Where you expect something in return? At least one of your values will be something that you give and receive. If you value respect, for example, then you can be respectful and also want respect in return. If you value helping people, you might expect people to help you in return. If you value love, you will give love and want to be loved also. This helps to bind your values to your expectations and personal standards. You want to give but also to get.

How did that feel? Good? Can you feel your life taking shape? Can you see your expectations and hopes taking form? Is the uncertainty you felt about life becoming clearer? Can you feel yourself taking control?

What Order Should the Other Values be in?

Is it crucial that the four subordinate values get placed into your Life Purpose statement in the exact same order? No, it doesn't matter what order they are in. The first value mentioned in your Life Purpose statement should be your #1 value, because it really starts off "I am...." – and the #1 value really speaks to who you are. The other four can be in any order, because they speak to what you like or want or try to be, but it is the #1 value that says, "I am...."

Some people argue that they have more than five values, and need to use more than five values in their Life Purpose statement – that's not a good idea. Having more than five becomes an excuse for not hunkering down and discovering which values are really most important. Plus it makes the Life Purpose statement cumbersome. Having so many values in it, defuses its impact.

Keep it Short and Succinct

If you have written your Life Purpose statement in accordance with Step 2, above, it will be quite brief. This is good. Don't be tempted to go charging ahead, adding lines with all sorts of picturesque phrases. If you did that, you might want to tighten it up. I think you will like your Life Purpose statement more if it is short and plain. For now, there is no need to go beyond your five most important values.

If you have added a number of words beyond what is required by Step #2, it may be difficult to make it any more brief than it is. By "tighten it up" I mean say the same thing in fewer words – say the same, not say less. You will like it better the more succinct it is.

As an example—

"... I am expressing myself freely and openly..." might become... *"...I express myself..."* — Using the active case instead of the passive case tightens it up – makes it more dynamic and reduces your statement by four words without saying less.

"... in all I choose to say, do and become..." might be written... *"...in all I choose to be..."* — You could trim three words from your Life Purpose statement. It would be shorter without saying less.

"... all my skills, talents and abilities..." could easily be *"... all my abilities..."* without saying less.

That's what I mean by being succinct. Of course, you will use words that resonate with you – the above were only to explain what I meant.

On this matter of being concise in your Life Purpose statement, we are only trying to capture your essence. That is your goal in this exercise — to capture your essence so completely there is nothing to be added, but also making it as compact as it can be. Just keep it simple. Place your five most important values in a line and string them together in a single sentence. In a moment, you will add color to create your full Life Purpose statement with all the inspiration and motivational power you want.

Here are two excellent examples of keeping your basic statement short.

I am ...confident... and ...adventure... and ...health... and ...humor... and ...honesty

"I am a confident person who loves adventure; I am grateful for my health and strive to maintain it; I see the humor in life and deal with life honestly, and expect others to be honest with me."

I am ...security... and ...fulfillment... and ...integrity... and ...making a difference... and ...someone to share life with

"I am a security-conscious person who seeks fulfillment in my life while maintaining my integrity; by making a difference and having someone to share my life with."

That was the exercise you worked on just now. How does this compare with what you wrote? Which do you like best?

Next we will add color, excitement and passion to your basic Life Purpose statement. You will make it inspiring, motivating and very personal by adding an icon to give visual aid to the words you have developed so far.

Step 3 – a Personal Icon

In the next step of the Life Purpose statement, you are to look about for a personal icon. By that I mean some item or concept that captures your essence. I cannot help you much with this because you must go deep inside yourself to find this icon.

Did you notice on my Life Purpose statement that it starts: "I am the dance of a candle flame...."? Not the candle, not the flame – I am the *dance.* That signified many things that are me—good things and some not-so-good, at times—playful, flippant, always moving, energetic, constant, sometimes softly waving but sometimes wavering and uncertain, illuminating but also casting shadows. Try to find something that conceptualizes you— something about which you could say, "If I wasn't a human being, THAT is what I would be."

Every Idea Can Spawn Another

I took ages finding my icon. In fact, I found my inspiration from an early Life Purpose statement. I thought of waving and wavering and dancing and imagined myself moving as if I was dancing and the movement became the playfulness of fire – I *was* the fire, then I was a flame, a candle flame.... It all flowed from inside because I have always been fascinated by fire, and have always been on the move. There is so much of me tied up in the dance of a candle flame, it seems uncanny.

This is why you have to dig so deep to find a personal icon. We don't really know ourselves very well—not as a whole. We know ourselves in little bits but rarely as a complex entity. We relate to things with bits of ourselves but not as a combination, never as a whole unit. As a consequence, some of our characteristics match a possible icon but others don't—until you find the one thing that matches on all counts, good and bad.

What is your favorite color? What sports do you favor? Which is the best movie you ever saw? Or favorite book? Is there a particular shape that resonates with you? Are there any hobbies that might serve. Any of these things may spark a thought that points to your personal icon.

Keep trying! You will find it. Or perhaps it might help to stop trying. Just think about who you are, what you are, how you are, and see what other things pop into your mind without effort.

Let's look at examples of what others have chosen for their icons. And there are some good ones. Hopefully these examples, and the reasons why these people chose their icons, will inspire you and help you find a suitable icon for yourself, too.

Cat Lover's Tiger Icon

Cat Lover's icon is a Tiger. She explains why:

"I have this tiger painting that is of a white tiger, in the jungle waiting for the storm to be over. You can see the drops of water on his fur... but the look on his face is he doesn't like the rain, but is waiting patiently for it to stop. I took one look at that painting, that was it! It was mine. I brought it home, I studied it and wrote down how that painting made me feel to look at it."

Weathering the storm
Patient
Loving, caring, protective of it's own family
Strong
Beautiful
Capable
Courageous
Willing to defend and fight if necessary.

"It is also because when I was going through a bad period of my life, I had a dream that was very lifelike... I dreamt that I was in the jungle, and was separated from my family. A tiger protected me in the jungle! Even knocking me over with his huge paw, and cuddling me like a huge furry person cuddling a teddy bear... he slept with his arm on me, to protect me. In the middle of the night a wild animal (a boar?) tried to attack us and he killed it. In the morning a hunting party found me, were going to shoot the tiger as they thought he was attacking me! I told them, NO, don't shoot him, he protected me all night long! The hunters lowered their guns. I said good-bye to the tiger, and it was like a deep spiritual connection... it was such a real dream... it was weird, but good. I was so overcome with that peaceful feeling I had from that dream, I made a tiger face pillow too. So Tigers represent strength to me... protective too... courage, etc... The tiger icon has been with me many years now..."

What a wonderful story. It is easy to see why a tiger was the icon of choice. This is the sort of thing that could become your icon, if you have a remarkable experience like this. Many people have something that appealed to them in childhood and which seems to follow them around as an adult. Maybe you had a favorite toy, or a special game you played, even an imaginary friend. One client's favorite color was orange and, when she looked around her house, she noticed that a common motif was a sunflower – on drapes and pillows and chinaware. This had already become her icon.

Your icon may arise from thinking of particular attributes you have and what things have those same characteristics. Are you joyful but melancholy? Silly and sad? Might a clown be your icon? What if you find yourself always solving puzzles, friends' problems, giving advice? Could a key be your icon? Or the turn of a key? What if you live life on the edge? If you like excitement, uncertainty, danger, even? Could your icon be the roll of the dice? – not the dice, necessarily, but the ROLL of the dice. Find that one thing or characteristic that speaks to your essence, and use it as your personal icon.

What are your personal characteristics? Are you energetic? Are you studious? Do you talk a lot? Write them down—

1. ....

2. ....

3. ....

4. ....

5. ....

6. ....

What "things" also have these attributes? ....

....

....

....

What could be your icon? ....

Paul's Hang Glider Icon

I had been doing this exercise with several people, and Paul had been following along with us. He said he had a lot of fun with this part of the process. He felt himself to be very visual and immediately saw the value in having a personal icon. He knew it would help him write his Life Purpose statement. Follow Paul's method and see if that helps you find your icon.

Firing quickly and just following his imagination, Paul first thought of words like, peak, pinnacle and summit. He remembered that when reading some personal development books, he had coined a phrase "Jumping off the Edge and Learning to Fly" and made that into a personal signature. It resonated with his feeling that sometimes you can't get all your ducks in a row before you step out, sometime you must act without being totally prepared, sometimes you have to just do it. Sometimes you have to step out in faith and face your fears with courage.

As he thought about this again, now, he envisioned someone on a hang glider standing on a cliff. The hang glider captured that phrase, "jumping off the edge and learning to fly."

It conjures up, for Paul, being on top of a mountain looking down. It makes him think of stepping out in faith. He thinks of exhilaration, what a rush this must be, such excitement. It depicts an ability to defy odds and defy gravity. It conjures up ideas of innovation, engineering, accomplishment, that there is always a way! But also of humility – a lone hang glider in the awesome expanse of the sky.

So much in one small image of a hang glider.

Apply Your Icon to Your Life Purpose

Paul had identified his most important values—

1. Happiness
2. Faith
3. Love
4. Authenticity
5. Fulfillment

He has found his personal icon — a hang glider.

He is now ready to rewrite his basic Life Purpose statement —

I am a hang glider ... who ....
Or—I am the energy of the hang glider. Or, how about: I am the sail of the hang glider ... who ...... (value 2) ....
(value 3) .... (value 4) ...., and .... (value 5)

Paul: *"I am a hang glider! When flying I am at my happiest. I can feel alone at times and I use this time to relax and recover. I can take that isolation as quiet time. But I can always see those I love around and know they are there for me, and they can see that I am there for them. Stepping off that cliff can be an act of faith and flying high lets me appreciate the awesome majesty of God and his creation. Flying high is a metaphor for my life of fulfillment."*

Notice how Paul wrote as if he was hang gliding while discovering his Life Purpose. In this fashion, the words are wrapped up into a complete and comprehensive statement.

In the next example, let's watch Greg doing the exercise from start to finish. We can see how Greg develops his values, Life Purpose and personal icon in one continuous flow.

Values – Icon – Life Purpose

See how it all comes together in the following example for Greg—

Greg's Most Important Values

1. Freedom to be me
2. Passion
3. Health
4. Fun
5. Creativity

Greg's Basic Life Purpose

I am... Free to be me *...with a...* Passion *...for...* Health, Fun *...and...* Creativity.

Greg's Personal Icon

The flight of the peregrine falcon

Greg's Life Purpose Statement

"I am the unfettered flight of a peregrine falcon. Infinite in possibility, boundless in depth, free to do as I wish, master of my domain. My only morality is whether my actions hurt others. I glide through life effortlessly, and revel in delight with the ease with which all I need comes to me. Taking time out to do a few tricks just for fun (and to impress my lady bird), I dive headfirst with absolute passion to pursue my desires and destiny. I maintain total health of mind body and soul for this is essential for my devastating speed. I was born to share my natural ingenuity and creativity with others, and am an exceptional teacher. I do not doubt my inner gifts of happiness, power and belief and let them loose on the world!"

Awesome!

Now rewrite *your* life purpose, as Paul and Greg did, this time using the characteristics of your personal icon.

Your personal icon: ....

Your Life Purpose statement: ....

....

....

....

....

....

Recap

(Fill in the blanks.)

So far, we have —

1. Discovered our most important values, which are:

....

....

....

....

....

2. Written our basic Life Purpose statement, which is:

....

....

....

....

3. Chosen our personal icon, which is:

....

4. Applied the characteristics of our personal icon to our basic Life Purpose statement. Which now looks like this:

....

....

....

....

....

....

Now is a good time for some wordsmithing. If you feel your Life Purpose statement doesn't flow or you have included some words that don't quite convey exactly what you mean, spending some time with a thesaurus will be very beneficial. You will find it clarifying your goals; it will suggest to you a mission.

To help tighten up your Life Purpose statement and help it flow, pick out three words you think don't quite say what you want to say, and then search your thesaurus for alternate words that are more expressive.

1. ....

    replace with ....

2. ....

    replace with ....

3. ....

    replace with ....

Next, pick out three phrases that you think are too long and cumbersome and write alternate phrases that are shorter and more flowing.

1. ....

    replace with ....

2. ....

    replace with ....

3. ....

    replace with ....

Make the changes and write your Life Purpose statement one more time, revised as above:

....

....

....

....

....

....

....

....

....

Doesn't that sound fabulous? Your Life Purpose statement is now motivating, inspirational and so utterly personal and true, you will wonder how you ever got along without it.

Next comes your mission statement.

YOUR MISSION STATEMENT

Your Mission Flows from Your Purpose

A mission statement comes after the Life Purpose statement. Discovering your Life Purpose guides you towards creating an appropriate mission, a mission that allows you to live your Life Purpose. Think of these two as a compass and a map: one sets the general direction, the other leads you from A to B.

Notice I keep saying "discover" purpose and "create" the mission. You don't create a purpose, you discover it. Now, it's true, your upbringing or conditioning may lead you to a purpose you no longer wish to follow. You can change it, but that is a different subject.

Paul came into this exercise with a mission already established. Some readers may also have a mission in place. So, the question becomes: Can you live your Life Purpose by fulfilling that mission? Because it is quite possible to carry out a mission but not satisfy your Life Purpose. There are many martyrs who do good deeds but are not happy in the process. A fulfilled life is one where you can follow your Life Purpose and also complete your mission.

Discovering your Life Purpose is therefore essential. Hold your mission in mind and state your inherent Life Purpose. Then the mission statement is a simple task of stating how following your Life Purpose will achieve the mission. Does that make sense?

For example, let's suppose your purpose is to be happy. You can be happy in all sorts of ways. Suppose you decide that living by the beach will make you happiest of all, so you make that your mission. Purpose: to be happy. Mission: to live by the beach.

Suppose your purpose is to contribute. You can contribute in many ways, but you decide to sponsor one hundred poor children. Purpose: to contribute to the world. Mission: sponsor one hundred poor children.

Suppose your purpose is to contribute more than you do already, and to do that you need to raise your income. Purpose: to contribute more. Mission: increase your income. Do you see how Life Purpose and mission work together?

If you have a mission statement already, write it down here. If you don't have a mission statement, but do have a general idea of what your mission is or will be, write that down.

....

....

....

....

....

A Life Purpose but No Mission

Question: What if you have a purpose – for example, to be happy – but you don't have a mission?

We had an example from before that was: Purpose: To Be Happy; Mission: Live on the Beach. But suppose you want to be happy but don't seem to know what or how to go about it. This seems to be a common problem with lots of people. They know they want to be happy but they don't know how to go about achieving it. They think happiness will just come to them.

The fact is, you need a mission in order to fulfill your Life Purpose. If you don't have a mission to accomplish, your Life Purpose lies dormant. You cannot just contribute until you have something or somebody to which you will contribute. You cannot just be free until you have some way to express that freedom. You cannot just be happy until you do something that makes you happy. A mission is imperative.

First, I can't tell you what will make you happy – only you can decide that. Possibly the reason you do not know what will make you happy is because happiness is tied up with everything else in your life and you are trying to clarify one piece without the rest. This is where a Life Purpose statement can be so helpful.

So many people try to create a Life Purpose statement without determining their values first. Have you done this exercise from the beginning? Discovering your values? Putting them into a basic Life Purpose, etc? If not, start at the beginning, do all the steps, and by the time you get back to this point, I'm sure you will have a clearer idea of what it is you want and how you can get it.

From your values and your Life Purpose, you will create a mission statement.

Create a Mission Statement

You have been working very hard up to this point. Is there an easy way to create a mission statement? There certainly is! You can copy the best mission statement that could possibly exist and rewrite it using words you have already incorporated in your Life Purpose statement. What is the best mission statement that could possibly exist? Before we answer that question, we must look at the intent of the mission statement.

You have discovered your Life Purpose in the work you have done up to now. This is something that continues throughout your whole life. A Life Purpose is something that can never be completed, but which goes on forever – like being happy, or contributing, or living in harmony or being free, and so on. It's not intended for these things to ever come to an end.

A mission, on the other hand, is something that will come to an end. It's a project. The intention is that it will be completed eventually. You will undertake this mission to achieve your purpose. It's the "why" behind the goal. (Goals are more likely to be accomplished if you have a powerful enough reason for achieving them.) You will buy a house on a beach because living on a beach will make you happy. Once you have the house, the mission is completed, while the happiness – your purpose – goes on.

On that basis then, a perfect mission statement must state something that will be achieved and which will be achieved within a certain time. The most perfect mission statement I have ever heard is one you will recognize —

"These are the voyages of the Starship Enterprise. Her five year mission: to explore strange new worlds, to seek out new life and new civilizations, to boldly go where no man has gone before."

Why is it so perfect? Because, having created it once, you don't have to think about it again until it is completed and you create a new one. If it is a family mission or the mission statement of a company, it is even more powerful. For example, if Captain Kirk and all the other senior officers were missing and the lowliest member of the crew stumbles upon a new world, he knows exactly what he must do – Explore it! He is even told HOW to explore it – Boldly!

Creating your mission statement, therefore, simply requires you to take the Star Trek mission statement and plug in words from your Life Purpose statement. As you will see, the format of the Star Trek mission lends itself to easy adaption. (You could, if you wish, borrow some other equally magnificent mission statement and adapt that to your purpose. I liked the Star Trek one.)

My Mission Statement

"This is my amazing voyage, where an exhilarating journey is everything and the destination nothing. My five year mission: to explore new wealth-attracting ventures, to seek out vibrant new people and new groups, to do challenging new things, to boldly go where I have not gone before."

Have fun with this, and explore the world of possibilities. There is more than one way to achieving your purpose – to be happy, to contribute, to be yourself – so explore the many ways and then pick one. Many people have difficulty with this, though, but really it doesn't matter what you pick. If your purpose is to contribute and you can contribute by giving to the Red Cross or donating to your local church, it really doesn't matter which one you choose, does it?

So, design a mission that will turn you on, fire you up, and get your juices flowing!

My mission is...

....

....

....

....

....

....

Cat Lover's Mission Statement

Cat Lover produced her mission statement, as follows. Notice how it flows from her previously stated values and life purpose:

"My five year mission is to move to a better location and fulfill more of my needs. Get employed in a job / career that I love – where I can contribute all my skills. To open myself up to finding a man and having a quality relationship with him.

To follow my heart and my dreams and allow new, positive experiences into my life. To do all this with passion, spirituality and the belief that it will come to me easily and effortlessly."

There! Isn't that wonderful? Isn't that worth waking up in the morning for? If you had a mission like that, congruent with your values and consistent with your Life Purpose, how could you fail to achieve it?

You could fail to achieve your mission – your goals – by having your values and your Life Purpose and your mission pulling in different directions. This is the reason it is essential to have your mission *flow out of your Life Purpose* and your Life Purpose to *flow out of your values*.

Nevertheless, each of us finds within ourselves something different and then expresses it in a different way. Some create a Life Purpose statement and a mission statement using a different approach and come to a different sounding result. That's fine, as long as the different parts are congruent – whatever works for you. The method I have described here has worked for me, and for many others, for many years.

But now we are going to add a new twist...

Your Personal Motto

We have reached the final step. The final step is the personal motto. Again, it's not as difficult as some of the earlier steps. Your personal motto might be something you heard or read, or someone else's motto duly adapted to your own purpose. Or, take a favorite phrase from your Life Purpose statement. I was captivated by a particular line in my mission statement, borrowed from Star Trek, and made that my personal motto:

"To boldly go where I have not gone before!"

You could do something similar, or you could come up with a new sentence of your own creation. Think of it as a company's tag line – the tagline of YOU, Inc.

Most companies have one – some long, some short – General Electric's, for example, used to be, "We bring good things to light." Currently, they are using, "Imagination at Work." Archer Daniels Midland Co. has "Resourceful By Nature" as their slogan. And, of course, there's Nike's famous, "Just Do It!"

What will be your motto?

Experiment! Try out a few ideas here:

....

....

....

....

....

In Conclusion

It took me about 3 months to get my Life Purpose statement, mission statement and personal motto completed! I found the more I looked at my values, the more they changed! When I thought I had them nailed down, and I wrote my basic Life Purpose statement, it didn't sound like me at all, so I had to start over, several times!

Then, when I got to the part where we dressed up the Life Purpose using adjectives of my icon, words failed me and I wore out my thesaurus (Thank heaven I *had* a thesaurus!) Just keep plugging away. Every confusing step is learning more about yourself and that will be very beneficial, indeed. Each step is a reminder of the wonderful, purposeful life you can have for the making.

For the record, now, write down the results of your efforts:

Your Most Important Values:

#1..

#..

#..

#..

#..

Your Personal Icon:

....

Your Life Purpose statement:

....

....

....

....

....

....

Your Mission Statement:

....

....

....

....

Your Personal Motto:

....

....

....

My approach in this chapter is one of the best ways of developing a Life Purpose statement, a mission statement and personal motto. It is an approach, I find, that is easily done in distinct steps and thus is easy to explain. It takes anyone following this route deep into their own thinking – which is necessary for a meaningful result.

A Life Purpose, based on and in agreement with your most important values, and a mission that carries you along on your life's journey, is a joy to live. It is as near a guarantee as you can get for success. It guides you to maintain focus and "to keep your eyes on the prize" – the prize of a wonderful, successful and fulfilling life.

I wish you an extraordinary life!

* * *

Random Acts of Kindness
by
Angela Christensen

RANDOM ACTS OF KINDNESS: AN INTRODUCTION

This chapter is about random acts of kindness, and the paying it forward principle. Before we discuss this topic, let's define what paying it forward means. Some people would think that you pay back a favor or kindness. But say the words "pay back" out loud and you are more than likely to think of the word "payback" as in "revenge."

I didn't use "pay back" because, even apart from the possible negative connotations, that term is not an appropriate description – it suggests the past rather than the future. And we want to affect the future. Paying it forward revolves around changing the future, not the past.

A few years ago, there was a movie entitled, "Paying it Forward." It tells the story of a 12-year-old boy, Trevor McKinney, who attempts to make the world a better place after his new social studies teacher gives him that chance. Young Trevor is troubled by his mother's alcoholism and fears of his abusive but absent father. An intriguing assignment from his teacher, Mr. Simonet, challenges Trevor to think of something that could change the world, and he is further challenged to put it into action. Trevor comes up with the idea of paying a favor not back, but forward, repaying good deeds not with payback, but with new good deeds done for three new people. Trevor's efforts to make good on his idea bring a revolution not only in the lives of himself, his mother and his teacher, but in those of an ever-widening circle of people completely unknown to him.

Paying it forward creates ripples in the pond. Ripples don't start from the outer circle, they start from within and spread outwards from there. Thus, one pays it forward into the future by helping someone, who helps someone, who in turn helps someone else.

You will come to see exactly how to pay forward a random act of kindness. So let's get started!

—Angela Christensen

RANDOM ACTS OF KINDNESS

What is a Random Act Of Kindness?

Random acts of kindness can help others and helps us as well. It's all about the pay it forward attitude. You just never know when some small thing you do can mean the world to someone else. The phrase, "pay it forward," may be new to some people although the concept will be familiar to most. It means doing a good deed for someone and paving the way by example for them to do a good deed, too. Everyone that does a random act of kindness is "paying it forward."

What is the "IT" Being Paid Forward?

Good will, caring, support, kindness, empathy, sincerity, compassion, humanity, joy, and gratitude: all those things are paid forward from one person to the next. Doing a random act of kindness brings hope, faith, trust, caring and gratitude to the recipient. It can also bring out those same good feelings in the person doing the random act of kindness.

Why are Random Acts of Kindness Important?

Doing random acts of kindness for others comes from the gratitude within ourselves. Having an attitude of gratitude is another tool you can utilize to ensure your success. Being grateful is part of the foundation on which you build your plans and goals. Successful people all display an attitude of gratitude, so the more random acts of kindness you do, the more gratitude you generate for yourself and others. Like ripples in a pond, it causes good acts to be carried on by others into the future. It spreads the seeds of hope, faith and generosity.

Who can You do Random Acts of Kindness for?

The answer is, for anyone and everyone. A random act of kindness can be done for someone you know or for a total stranger. The different acts of kindness are limited only by your imagination. It doesn't matter who we are, how much money we have – we're all able to do some act of kindness for others when it isn't expected. We can pass along a compliment or a smile. Do something as simple as holding a door for someone, or give a dime in the grocery store line if someone doesn't have quite enough.

Who can you think of, right now, for whom you can do a random act of kindness?

1 ....

2 ....

3 ....

4 ....

5 ....

Random Acts of Kindness Help Foster a Sense of Community

Random acts of kindness are so special because, let's face it, life can get quite impersonal. We use e-mail so much that our social skills are more apt to be honed for online use. As we embrace technology more, some argue that we are drifting away from one another, that we are losing our sense of "community." The smallest act of kindness can really brighten someone's day and can even be what turns them around. When a person is depressed, having an act of kindness done for them may just be what restores their faith in mankind. It helps them feel they are important too, and a part of a bigger community than they may realize.

To give you an example: I had moved to a new city and was very lonely there. I had only my fiancé and his daughter for company. One weekend, we were holding a garage sale when an elderly couple arrived. They said they had a set of dressers they wanted to get rid of. I told them we were looking for some ourselves and if they planned on having a garage sale, to let us know and we would come to their event as well. A few hours later, it was starting to rain. It was time to close it down for the day anyway. As we were putting stuff away, a truck arrived. It was the elderly man from earlier in the afternoon.

He said to me, "Excuse me, Miss. Would you like to come take a look at this dresser set in the back of the truck? If you want them, they are yours for free."

"Thank You so much... this is so unexpected, are you sure I can't give you some money for them?" I asked.

"No Ma'am, just happy to know that someone gets them who can use them," he said.

I was so filled with gratitude that day. Here I had been feeling sorry for myself and, quite unexpectedly, a stranger appeared with something I needed. It reminded me to stop focusing on the negative things I was feeling. It reminded me that there are good people everywhere. It was exactly what I needed. That simple act of kindness made me feel less alone and more a part of the community I had moved to.

I often find ways of giving to others or doing random acts of kindness for others. It's all part of being spiritual. I believe that random acts of kindness and gratitude are very closely intertwined, and also linked to the law of attraction: "Like attracts like." It is part of the law of karma as well: "What goes around comes around." When you do good things for others, it comes right back to you – often in surprising ways.

What kindness could you do for someone, right now?

1 ....

2 ....

3 ....

4 ....

5 ....

How "Paying It Forward" Helped my Family in a Crisis

Through my volunteer work, I find people for whom I can do random acts of kindness all the time. Much of my past non-paying work has been helping victims of crime and being a victim's advocate. I was a team captain for a program that helped fire evacuees. My mother was a victim's assistance worker for a police department. We both held these volunteer positions for years. During the course of our volunteer work we did many random acts of kindness for complete strangers.

What goes around comes around! One cold winter day, my brother was involved in a major propane explosion. He suffered second and third degree burns to over thirty-five percent of his body. Suddenly, people were coming from everywhere to help my brother. They wanted to help this man they had read about in the newspapers and had seen on the Six O'clock News. One man came into my brother's hospital room, and gave him five hundred dollars cash. People gave donations of clothing and household items to him. One person offered to give him a trailer to live in. Some companies even offered to give him free internet when he got out of the hospital. It was as if all the good deeds my mom and I had done for others were now coming back to our family a hundred-fold. So when you think you are doing these good deeds just for others, little do you know that you are also helping yourself and loved ones down the road.

How Does Doing Random Acts of Kindness Tie into Being Successful?

Who do you think will be more sought out for promotions and advancement, and receive recognition from their peers? Who would be welcomed into other peoples' inner circles? A person who is more self-focused and only doing for themselves, or a person who thinks more expansively and shows more caring for all people? Who would you rather have as a boss? What kind of person do you want to be perceived as being?

People who give of themselves are naturally more capable of inspiring others and of carrying an organization's vision into the future. People who care about the consequences of their words and actions are going to be perceived as more approachable, even-tempered and inspiring. They show more leadership skills than someone who acts selfishly and climbs the corporate ladder at other people's expense.

Why is This an Important Attribute to Develop?

Very wealthy and socially conscious people tithe money to worthy causes. If you start off your goals with the stated intention of being able to help others, the law of karma and the law of attraction say it is more likely to come to you. For some people this is a spiritual belief and is held close to them like a sacred truth. Others believe they have a responsibility to help others, foster community, and are socially conscious. Yet others do it because they believe that what you reap is what you sow. Like attracts like. If you are helping others whenever you can, it will come back to you multiplied. Like any other skill, it can be nurtured and developed.

Do You Need to Believe in the Law of Karma or Law of Attraction for This to Work?

No. You don't have to believe in either concept for them to work. I believe they are simply universal truths. You can debate their validity in your life or you can set about using them to your greatest advantage. You may think that is against all spiritual beliefs, but it isn't. For example, using a gratitude journal helps you focus on all you have, making you more willing to give, which brings more to you. Which in turn gives you even more to be grateful for. It is cyclical. The more you give, the more you get in return. Gratitude and random acts of kindness are all a part of the recipe for success. Look at the people you consider to be successful. Chances are they all carry that same attitude of gratitude and spread random acts of kindness. More will be said about the gratitude journal in the chapter on Gratitude.

You may be thinking that doing random acts of kindness is a great thing to do but wonder how to get started. Well, here are some ideas to get you started ranging from small to large... in no particular order.

1) If you encounter a rental shopping cart, leave a quarter in the shopping cart for the next person who comes along. They may be busy with children, or may not have a quarter. Or someone will come along looking for loose carts with quarters in them, who really needs them.

2) Call a salesperson or cashier by name – just look at their nametag. It makes a person feel good to be acknowledged.

3) Fill out a positive customer comment card for a salesperson who gives you good customer service. It gets recorded on their personnel file. You will make them smile from ear to ear.

4) Hold a door open for someone.

5) Smile at someone and say hello as you pass them on the street.

6) If you see someone running for the bus, and you are also getting on the bus ahead of them, tell the driver someone is running to catch up.

7) Give someone a sincere compliment.

8) Put your pennies in the little dish at the cashier's line: "take a penny, leave a penny."

9) Send a get well card to someone you know who is not feeling well.

10) Stop by a nursing home and talk to some of the residents. Listen to their stories. Perhaps offer to teach a class or call bingo.

11) If you stay in a hotel, leave a tip for the maid on the pillow along with a thank you note.

12) Pay for the next person's meal or dry cleaning when you go through the drive through. Or pay the bridge toll for the person behind you, too.

13) Do you see a city worker or crew working out in the cold in front of your house or apartment? Bring them some coffee or hot chocolate to warm them up.

14) When shoveling your own sidewalk, also shovel the sidewalk of someone in your neighborhood who is elderly, or who you know is not feeling well or unable to shovel their own sidewalk.

15) Wave people in front of you in traffic.

16) Hold the elevator door open for someone.

17) Run an errand for someone.

18) Write a nice thank you note on the receipt for your waiter or waitress along with leaving them a nice tip.

19) Be a Secret Santa to someone. Perhaps a family you know needs money for food or gifts during the holidays. You can also buy new items and donate them at different places, such as department stores, food banks, the Salvation Army, churches, etc.

20) Donate your used clothing and household items to charity.

21) Buy a book for a friend that you think they would like or can use.

22) Offer to baby-sit for a neighbor.

23) Did you hear of someone suffering a loss of their house due to a house fire? Donate money, clothing, household items, furniture, toys.

24) Pick three random names out of the phone book. Send them ten dollars each, and explain it is a random act of kindness. Do not put a return address on the envelopes.

25) Tell emergency workers that you see – police, fire and ambulance workers – how much you appreciate the jobs they do for your community.

26) Donate your old non-working vehicle to charity. They get the money for parts and scrap metal, and you get a tax receipt.

27) Put food and water out for stray animals in the wintertime, or water in the summertime.

28) Better yet find a home for any stray animals you see in your neighborhood.

29) If you are approached by a street person for money, offer to buy them a hot meal and buy it for them. You will ensure that they have had a hot meal that day.

30) Hand out kindness cards to people you meet. You can make them yourself, or find some online to print out. They have sayings on them like "You have a beautiful smile.... pass it on!"

31) If you know of someone new to your neighborhood, call Welcome Wagon and they will come round to give your new neighbor goodies, coupons and information about the neighborhood.

32) Bring your co-workers or boss a coffee, some donuts or even some candies.

33) Buy a bouquet of flowers and walk down the street. For every person who comments on them – give them a flower!

34) Fill out some Christmas Cards for all your favorite local merchants and hand them out the next time you go shopping.

35) Give your local postal carrier a Thank You card or Christmas card and put five or ten dollars in it.

36) Offer to give a friend or co-worker a ride in bad weather, if you know they take public transportation.

37) Offer to look after your neighbor's home when they go away on holidays, or to look after their pets.

38) If you see your neighbor's garbage cans or lids being blown away, put them in a spot where they will not get blown away but still be easy to find.

39) If you see a neighbor's mail or newspapers piling up, take them in until you see your neighbors have returned. Then give them their mail and papers. You may prevent their house from being broken into.

40) Offer to help a senior with their yard work.

41) Offer to help someone with their recycling.

42) Do you have a lot of pop or water bottles? Call your local Boy Scouts or Girl Guides to see if they want them for the bottle deposits. If not, call your local schools or youth organizations. Almost all of them need extra money and will be happy to take them off your hands.

43) Do you know someone who is homesick and wishes they could be with their family at Christmas? Give them some money or buy them a ticket home, if you can afford it.

44) Learn how to say "Happy Holidays" or "Happy New Year" in a few different languages. If you know someone is Asian, wish them "Gung Hoi Fat Choy" which means "Happy New Year!" It will bring a smile to their faces.

45) Give up your seat on the bus to someone who is older than you, or has children or lots of packages with them.

46) Feed the birds in the winter months and put out water. Keep it ice-free when it's very cold.

47) Buy some helium balloons and walk around the mall. Give one to every person who comments on them.

48) Buying some small gift for your friends' or relatives' pets is always appreciated at Christmas time, even if it is a can of food or a bag of treats. Animals also appreciate these little gifts.

49) Offer to help a senior citizen in your neighborhood to put lights up on their house or in their yard for Christmas.

50) Offer to take Christmas decorations and lights down for the seniors in your neighborhood. Or offer to recycle Christmas trees for them.

Add a couple of your own...

51) ....

52) ....

There you have fifty-two ideas of how you can do a random act of kindness. Throughout the course of the day, you will see opportunities to be kind to someone.

When we offer these gifts of kindness to others, it cheers them up and can restore their faith in mankind. A small thing like a random act of kindness goes a long way. Feel stuck for something to do still? Think back. Someone has surely done a small random act of kindness for you. There are always ways of "paying it forward." You are limited only by your imagination and quick problem solving skills. Be a part of the pay it forward revolution. It will come back to you ten-fold, when you or your loved ones least expect it.

Where are the Best Places to Find Someone in Need of a Random Act of Kindness?

Successful people, like the famous Composer/ Arranger / Producer David Foster, start foundations to assist children in need of organ transplants. Donald Trump helps children through the Elizabeth Glazier Pediatric Aids Foundation. So look to your local hospitals, care centers, shopping malls, doctors' offices, places of employment, youth organizations, children's hospitals, vet clinics... the list is endless. Most of the suggestions here cost you nothing except for your time. Some of these ideas are very low cost to do. Others, depending on your resources and income, can be as large as you want to make them. The principle isn't about how much monetary value your act of kindness has, but that the act of kindness comes from your heart and reaches out to another person's heart.

That, after all, is the greatest gift we can give: the validation to others that they are all valuable human beings. The recipients of your acts of kindness will feel grateful, special and appreciated. The law of attraction will ensure that what you sow is what you reap. So don't be surprised when others do random acts of kindness for you, but remember to pay it forward. You never know when someone close to you, or maybe even you, will need the kindness of strangers some day. As the saying goes "But for the Grace of God, there go I..."

Know that when you do a random act of kindness for someone, it WILL come back to you. Perhaps on rare occasions, you might find that your act of kindness wasn't appreciated. Or you may feel that you helped the wrong person. Take heart though. Know that your good intentions were set into motion and that they DO make a difference. Just because you can't see the results right away, doesn't mean your random act of kindness doesn't count. It does count. Random acts of kindness, paying it forward, being grateful, they all result in attracting more towards you. Always remember that.

If you want more information on this concept, simply search for the terms "pay it forward" or "random acts of kindness" in any internet search engine. You will see many active organizations dedicated to this concept. I wholeheartedly encourage you to explore this concept further.

Kindness is something we should never save for only ourselves and our loved ones. Spread the happiness and appreciation all over. For when you give so freely of yourself, you also open yourself up to receiving as well. I know I will always be grateful for all the strangers that helped my brother when he was in the hospital for a month. Those memories still touch our family's hearts today, as much as they did at the time it happened. Remember to add this tool to your success kit. It is part of the recipe of success that many others have used and continue to use. It works for Oprah Winfrey, Donald Trump, David Foster, Maya Angelou and many more. It works for me, too, and it can work for you as well. May you always be blessed to give and receive random acts of kindness.

* * *

Gratitude
by
Angela Christensen

GRATITUDE: AN INTRODUCTION

I saw an Oprah Winfrey show many years ago, and she said she kept a gratitude journal. Maya Angelou was on that show, and she had been the one to teach Oprah to keep a gratitude journal. Watching that show inspired me to do the same.

Oprah and Maya Angelou explained how being in a constant state of gratitude transformed both their lives. Being in a constant state of gratitude was one of their most important success strategies. I thought, if it worked for them, it could work for me! I took Oprah's challenge and made it into my own. I started keeping a gratitude journal. That was about twelve years ago. Now, it is a way of life for me to be grateful every day.

No matter how bad I feel, when I write in my gratitude journal I feel better. There are some days it feels harder than others to find something to be grateful for, not because I have had a bad day, but because my day has simply been uneventful. I have found that the more gratitude I openly express to all the people in my life, the more I get back. But the reason I express it is because expressing gratitude to others helps validate them and lift their spirits too! It helps pay the "attitude of gratitude" forward.

I have learned how important it is to validate others, from my time in volunteer work. I learned that it is important to strengthen others, as we also strengthen ourselves in doing so, and we do this by being empathetic, caring and generous. These traits have served me well. I can remember the lean days, when I didn't have much. It didn't upset me that I lived in subsidized housing, had second-hand furniture and second-hand clothes; I was grateful for all of it! Because I couldn't work at a paying job in those days, I chose to volunteer a lot of my time. This allowed me to get into a better mindset.

One of those volunteer jobs was being a Team Captain for a program that helped fire evacuees. I would help people for three solid days after they had been evacuated from their burned down homes and apartment buildings. Now this may seem like really depressing work to some people. Not to me though. Sure, it was brutally hard to look someone in the eyes and say, "I am so sorry but everything that you owned is gone due to the fire." They would break down, and then it was my job to help them pick up the pieces of their life again. My team and I had only three days to do that with each person we dealt with.

It was a hard job to do, but very rewarding. It was rewarding that sometimes we were able to help people so that they were better off after the fire than they were before it. The gratitude those people expressed to us volunteers will live on in my heart forever! Some days I would come home from dealing with an evacuated family, look around my small seven hundred square foot apartment, and break down and cry. Cry out of remorse for the evacuees and pray that things would get better for them. Pray to be an instrument of good for them in any way I could, and cry out of pure gratitude for all that I had. Doing that volunteer job for over two years kept me ever grateful and humble.

My circumstances in life have changed since then, but I remain as grateful today as I was then, if not more so. To me gratitude is a lifestyle choice. It is about the way I think, feel and act. It is about my every action and reaction. It is about paying it forward every chance I have by doing random acts of kindness to help others. It is about being an ear to listen to a friend. It is about counting my blessings for every reminder I get that my life has improved so much. It is about being as grateful for the small things as it is for the big things. For me, it is now also a part of my success tool kit.

For some people, gratitude is just another word. To me, it is a way of life.

—Angela Christensen

GRATITUDE

What is Gratitude?

Gratitude is more than a feeling, it is an attitude: one of abundance, feeling blessed and remaining humble. Gratitude is about counting one's blessings, of being grateful for the things in your life, both big and small. Being grateful helps you to focus on all the positive things in your life. If you are grateful for what you have, there is no room for jealousy. Too many people are jealous of what others have and wish they could have the same things. They could, if only they would adopt an "attitude of gratitude."

Gratitude encompasses my spiritual beliefs, random acts of kindness, empathy, sincerity, honesty, caring and generosity. The world would be a better place if everyone felt and practiced gratitude more frequently. When you make a conscious decision to show your gratitude towards others throughout your entire day, you enrich your life and the lives of those around you. Some of the most successful people in the world stay in an "attitude of gratitude" all the time. People like Oprah Winfrey have used this to not only attain success, but to maintain their success.

How can you practice gratitude? We'll look at that more in depth now.

How Does One Practice Being Grateful?

Adopt an "Attitude of Gratitude"

Keep a gratitude journal. Stick with it. In no time at all, you will feel the effects that being grateful can generate in your life. It starts acting like a pattern interrupt. Instead of being jealous of someone else, you will feel joy for them. Instead of wishing you had more, you will feel blessed for how much you already have. Gratitude opens up our hearts, our minds, our eyes, our ears and our spirits in so many ways.

How Can You Start Feeling Gratitude?

Do you know the feeling of being hugged when you really need it? That is partly what it feels like. Do you remember the feeling you get when you listen to the radio and hear an old song played that brings back good memories? That is also what it can feel like. Do you know what it is like when a puppy licks your face, or expresses its happiness to see you? That is gratitude. Gratitude is deeply connected to love, to feeling – to being.

How Does Gratitude Make You Feel?

Gratitude makes me feel open, loving, centered, helpful, caring, warm and spiritual. It is a feeling that comes from my heart, not my head. You may feel it in other ways, but that is how it feels to me.

How does Gratitude make YOU feel?

....

....

....

....

How Can You Start Practicing Gratitude?

It is very easy to do. Take two minutes before you go to bed every night to write down three things you are grateful for that day. You can write more if you want, but always write a minimum of three things you are grateful for. Do that every single day. It is as simple as that. With every entry you make into your gratitude journal, you are conditioning your mind to be more grateful. The beautiful part of writing them down is that you get to re-experience those grateful feelings at the end of your day too. For me, I love being able to fall asleep with those thoughts of gratitude still in my mind and in my heart.

When Will You See the Results of Feeling More Grateful?

That all depends. For me, I guess it took a month or two to become a real habit, even though I had always felt a large amount of gratitude in my life. But it was about six weeks or so, before I felt as though a higher power was acknowledging me and all my thoughts of gratitude. You don't necessarily have to believe in a higher power for gratitude to work in your life.

Why Does Being Grateful Work?

Think of gratitude as being a part of the law of attraction and the law of karma. What you think about, you talk about. What you talk about, you bring about. So if in the back of your mind, you are always feeling grateful, then you will always find something new to be grateful for. What you reap is what you sow. So if you spread seeds of hope, validation, empathy, sincerity, generosity, compassion and gratitude, then it all comes back to you in greater abundance..

Can I prove it to you scientifically? No. But can I prove it to you in how I feel I have changed as a person, from using this technique? Oh yes! Do I know it works? Yes, absolutely. Maintaining an "attitude of gratitude" also works in tandem with "paying it forward" and doing "random acts of kindness" as well. They all work together to create a richer life.

Will it Really Work for Me, Too?

You have nothing to lose by taking a couple of minutes every day, to write down what you are grateful for. You have a lot to gain. By doing this, it has helped me realize that patience is indeed a virtue, that God's delays are not God's denials. It has taught me that caring from my heart and being open to others opens them up to me as well. I have learned that it makes no difference how much money you have or where you live, but the more you are grateful for, the more you are given to be grateful for. I have seen how random acts of kindness have helped crack open the toughest non-believing hearts with feelings of gratitude. When they see that complete strangers can and do help others, I have seen how this can help restore people's faith in mankind. Oprah Winfrey and Maya Angelou were right and it has changed my life. If you try it, I am confident it will help change your life, too. You will be programming yourself for success in every area of your life.

What is one thing you feel grateful for right now?

....

How Does Being Grateful Work?

I know that gratitude is a result of our actions. Gratitude is a feeling. Gratitude is an attitude. The more grateful you are, the more the Universe opens up and showers you with more to be grateful for. That may sound farfetched to the scientific types, and that is okay. Not everything can be explained. Science cannot explain how love is so necessary to all of us. Psychologists and the like can explain the how's and why's of it, but they can't explain to us what it actually *feels* like. It is something that we have to feel for ourselves, to truly understand its impact on us. The same holds true for being grateful. It isn't something that will be identical for everyone. Every person will feel gratitude in a way that is unique to them. What I can tell you is this: try it! Try using an attitude of gratitude and see if it doesn't make you feel better. If nothing else, you gain yet one more tool to add to your success kit!

What is another thing you feel grateful for right now?

....

How Becoming More Grateful Helped Me

I was suffering from serious depression and severe panic attacks when I started keeping my gratitude journal. I can tell you from personal experience how much it helped with my depression and panic. You see, *Gratitude is joy and is the opposite of depression.* So, if you are depressed, try it! Try writing down some of the things you can feel grateful for. Keep at it. Soon you will see the results. As you look around, you will see more and more to be grateful for. You will see how it helps with your depression, anxiety and worries. I can speak from personal experience that it helped in all those areas for me.

What is a Gratitude Journal?

A gratitude journal is a place to keep all your thoughts on what you are grateful for. You can record the things you are grateful for in an actual book, or at an online site, or in a blog. The means by which you keep a gratitude journal is not nearly as important as being grateful. Some people feel more connected when writing by hand, while others find it easier to do on their computer or online.

A gratitude journal is for recording all the things that you are grateful for that day. You write down at least three things you are grateful for every day in your gratitude journal. It doesn't matter if the things you are grateful for are big or small, each one counts. It is the practice of being grateful that is the main key. Writing down what we are grateful for conditions our mind to think automatically from an "attitude of gratitude." And when you write down what you feel blessed for that day, it keeps you inspired. It helps you to see you are not alone. It helps you maintain a positive focus. It helps you achieve a positive mindset and sets the stage for other good things to come to you, easily and effortlessly.

Write down a third thing you feel grateful for right now.

....

Meditating Before Writing in Your Gratitude Journal Can Help

You may want to meditate prior to writing in your journal. I don't, because I can get into that feeling instantly. However, I know many people who do meditate first. Find a place to be peaceful and relax. Empty your mind. Visualize a flame of a candle. Breathe deeply and place your hand over your heart. Focus on your breathing until it feels calm and steady and you feel ready to move on. When you are ready, think back over your day and choose something to be grateful for. Focus on that thought. Intensify that thought. Really feel what it means to you. Keep breathing deeply. Remember that feeling so when you need to, you can recall how gratitude feels to you. Feel the calming effect it has. Feel how peaceful and relaxed you are. Do you feel the weight of all your blessings today? Does your heart feel full of love?

Good! Now take a few more minutes to write down what you are specially grateful for today.

....

....

....

Take My Ninety Day Challenge.

Instructions

1. Buy a notebook that appeals to you. Large or small. It can have a cloth covering, or a design. Pick one that inspires you to write in it. This will be your gratitude journal.

2. On the inside page write down "__your name__ Gratitude Journal."

3. On the second page, date when your gratitude journal begins.

4. If you want, you can also add a brief mission statement in the front of your book. E.g. "To write down at least three things per day that I am grateful for." Then add your personal motto.

5. Add to your gratitude journal daily, write more than three things if you can — but always a minimum of three things — for which you are grateful that day. Don't worry if your entries sound repetitive. Expressing your gratitude is what is important.

I am sure you will look back over what you have written and truly see how much you really do have to be grateful for. Keep with it; it works!

To help get you started, I will share with you some of my own entries from my gratitude journal. I hope you will see that not everything has to be major. Gratitude in any amount, for any reason, is still a good reason to write about it. I hope these examples will help you to come up with some things to write about too. Below is a sample of what seven days worth of my gratitude journal looks like.

Day One

Today I am grateful to be reminded I have choices.
Today I am grateful to be reminded to read some good books I have.
Today I am grateful for all the connections with people I am making here.
Today I am glad that I am starting to feel better...

You see from the above example, I am grateful for books, other people and my health... a variety of things.

What are you reminded of that you can feel grateful for?

....

....

Day Two

Today I am grateful for a FULL day today.
Today I am grateful to be adjusting my hours again!
Today I am grateful to be playing catch up with my friends in real life too.
Today I am grateful my body is starting to feel better.
Today I am grateful for friendships new and old!
Today I am grateful for all the great advice I have been getting here...
Today I am grateful for all the motivation building in me now!
Wow...!!

This day's example is more personal, and in tune as to my mood that day. I felt busy and productive, helpful and being helped.

What are you reminded of that you can feel grateful for?

....

....

Day Three

Today I am grateful to have such great help from so many people!
Today I am grateful for the notes of encouragement I have received.
Today I am grateful for the e-mails of encouragement, too!
Today I am grateful to be getting my home decorated and more to my liking – expressing more of myself and making my home my refuge!

Today I am grateful to see my cats acting all silly.. really playing a lot today!
Today I am grateful for a warm home... when it is so cold outside.
Today I am grateful to be volunteering and taking on more duties.
Today I am grateful for a bit of a break and to watch some TV tonight.
Today I am grateful to feel so motivated!
Today I am grateful to be learning so much at the moment...

This entry also has a lot of variety. A warm home, to watch TV, to be learning, etc. Can you find something similar to be grateful for?

What are you reminded of that you can feel grateful for?

....

....

Day Four

Today I am grateful for all the motivation I feel. I haven't felt this energized for a long time!
Today I am grateful for the laughter, gratitude, caring and friendships here!
Today I am grateful that all the books I have ordered will be here soon! I can't wait to read Corinne's books, and Coach's book too!! Wooooohooooo!
Today I am grateful for the comedy show I watched before going to sleep. Nothing like a good dose of laughter to keep you happy and positive! Laughter really is the best medicine!
Today I am so grateful for the time I have to work on my books. I am not unemployed... I am a writer working on my books!

In this entry I am grateful for laughter, books, friendships. An entry doesn't have to follow a general theme from day to day. It does help if you write down something that is specific to you for that day though.

What are you reminded of that you can feel grateful for?

....

....

Day Five

Today I am grateful my sore hip is somewhat better. I need to get out again tomorrow while the weather is still nice!
Today I am grateful I am not snacking as bad as I was...
Today I am grateful for the life I lead... and I want to always remember that!

A day when I only made three entries, which is fine. If you are really tired it is okay to not push yourself to write more than three things for the day.

What are you reminded of that you can feel grateful for?

....

....

Day Six

Today I am grateful to be reminded of all the people that have helped me on my path...
Today I am grateful I can help others along their paths too.

Today I am grateful for a warm house, fridge full of food, and bed to sleep in.

This had not been a bad day for me, but a rather uneventful day. So I chose to write about things that I am always grateful for, rather than anything that happened that day in particular.

What are you reminded of that you can feel grateful for?

....

....

Day Seven

Today I am so grateful for the words of encouragement I am getting, as I set out to get published!

Today I am grateful for the time here at home, to be able to do my research and find out what I need to know in order to get published.

Today I am grateful for the resources to buy all my friends books! I am going to have quite the collection!

Today I am grateful I made it to the post office before it turns really cold again. It sucks to not be able to get out as much as I would like. But I am very grateful for days like today, when I do get out of the house.

Today I am grateful to talk to my mom last night.

Today I am grateful for the friendships I am making.

Today I am grateful I am re-connecting with my son again. Slow baby steps to progress!

Today I am grateful to be getting all my poems typed up – 80 down, 170 more to go!

Today I am grateful for all the abundance I have in my life...

Today as always I am grateful for my two furry friends who make me laugh so hard at times, with their silly antics.

This entry had a lot of different things I was grateful for that day. Some days you just keep coming up with more and more things to be grateful for!

What are you reminded of that you can feel grateful for?

....

....

(End of Samples)

How Do I Properly Fill Out My Gratitude Journal?

There is no right or wrong way to write in your gratitude journal. Some people, like myself, also use it as a diary of sorts, to keep it "real," so they can chart their progress when they go back and re-read their entries. Other people like to write their gratitude entries more like positive affirmations. Both ways work. What I can tell you is write from your heart. That is where our gratitude lives within us – in our hearts.

Some Simple Suggestions for Starting a Gratitude Journal

You will notice that most of the time I always start my entries the same way: "Today I am grateful for..."

Adopt a way of starting off your entries, too. Make it something personal to you, that feels right for you. It will help you to be consistent, and it helps re-wire the brain to notice gratitude in the same manner every time. It also acts as a pattern interrupt, especially on days when things aren't going so smoothly. Start off your entries with the same wording and, with every entry you make in your gratitude journal, you will be helping to condition your mind for success.

How Gratitude Primes our Brains for Success

Gratitude helps us recognize what we need to learn so we should be grateful for both our successes and our challenges. Challenge allows us to recognize what our strengths and weaknesses are and gives us a chance to experience success. So, if you condition your mind to see things through a filter of gratitude, you are ensuring a more positive mindset, and this in turn helps you maintain your focus. It will help you keep your eyes on the prize.

Using a tool such as a gratitude journal works from the inside out and guides the unfolding of your Life Purpose. Being grateful is as important as having confidence and persistence, or having faith. When you develop your attitude of gratitude, you are building a stronger foundation, on which you can successfully build all your dreams into reality. In this way you fulfill your Life Purpose. It worked for Oprah Winfrey and Maya Angelou, and I know it works for me, too. It will work for you. Give it a try!

I hope these examples help you to come up with some wonderful entries for your own gratitude journal. Remember gratitude is joy: made up of the little things that make you feel better, make you smile and bring you comfort. Celebrate your moments of gratitude for a few minutes every day by keeping a gratitude journal. It is time well spent. You will truly be amazed at the improvements it will bring into your life. One day when you look back at your earliest entries, you will be surprised by what you see. You will realize how far you have come and how much progress you have made. You will see how being more grateful has made a difference in the pursuit of your goals, in your personal relationships and how it has added to your success. People like Oprah Winfrey and Maya Angelou maintain their "attitudes of gratitude" to sustain the success they have achieved. You can too!

I learned a long time ago to write down at least three things I am grateful for every day. Join in and remind yourself what you are grateful for today. I am grateful to be living my life and to be in charge of my own destiny. What a great feeling! No one could have told me how good this would feel. It all started many years ago for me, when I started getting grateful for all the good things in my life. I am so grateful I learned about gratitude. It has changed my life for the better.

Today, I am reminded to be grateful for experiences and the growth I get from them, no matter how frustrating, depressing or anxiety filled they are. I am also grateful for the good moments, too, of course. Those moments hold such powerful feelings of gratitude.

Count your blessings! Be grateful for all that you have! Stop being resentful, angry, or depressed over not having enough! Open yourself up to having more, by first being grateful for all you already have. More will come to you that way. Then acknowledge all you have and start thinking from a place of abundance. You already have so much. You already have abundance! You just aren't recognizing it.

You *can* accomplish all your lofty goals. It only takes two minutes a day to re-wire your brain into an "attitude of gratitude." Every successful person has an attitude of gratitude within their souls. They also have something else in common: a desire to pay it forward. This desire ensures that you will bring gratitude into your own life and into others' lives as well. It isn't something that just happens in movies. You can make it work for you, too!

Best wishes, and may you always be blessed and have many things to be greateful for.

* * *

Taking Action

TAKING ACTION

This last chapter is to wrap up what we have been doing in the previous chapters. We think it would be beneficial for you, the reader, to know how we were before our own transformations took place. Angela had a life-changing experience doing Frederick's Life Purpose exercise. Frederick felt the life-changing effect of Angela's Attitude of Gratitude and Random Acts of Kindness. How did these changes come about?

Angela has always been outgoing. She comes from a family of entertainers and has appeared on stage as a magician's assistant. Frederick always took a while to get to know people and is generally quite reserved. Even so, Frederick was more aggressive, while Angela, having dealt with many struggles and abuse in her past, was more eager to avoid controversy.

Clearly, we are very different people. Angela comes from a victim mentality turned survivor, turned thriver. Frederick comes from an adversarial business background. We come with two different approaches to life. Reading about how two such different people overcame their individual obstacles by discovering Life Purpose, becoming grateful, etc. may help you apply these concepts to your own life.

You may be wondering what made us think we could write a book together? What was it that made us think we could cooperate in this fashion? What similarities did we share, even though we are so different and come from such diverse backgrounds? From what common ground did we start?

As has been mentioned, our paths first crossed on an internet discussion forum. Angela admits that initially she felt intimidated by Frederick. He seemed older, wiser and was a married business man. Angela is a single woman who recently left yet another bad relationship. She remained wary of his posts, until Frederick wrote about discovering his Life Purpose.

Meanwhile, Frederick paid little attention to Angela's approach to life because he found it trivial, but became captivated by her experience in conflict resolution. And throughout it all, Angela kept slipping in references to gratitude. Even in the worst of times. Angela was always able to find something to be grateful for.

After we each recognized that we both had some interesting attributes, we discovered that we are both members of Toastmasters International, the worldwide public speaking and leadership organization. We understood right away what the other was experiencing by attending those meetings, and how each was using the lessons learned.

Frederick had been a Toastmaster for three years while Angela was a new member. Nevertheless, Angela comes to Toastmasters as an experienced speaker, having studied broadcasting and done some previous work in the field in front of a camera, while Frederick has spent a lifetime avoiding the limelight!

Joining Toastmasters International was for Frederick, the result of deciding to start a new life after retiring from his former demanding, technical career. Following the creation of his Life Purpose statement, Frederick decided to become a Business Mentor – which is rather like life coaching but focusing on a client's business life. To be a success in this field, it is clearly an asset to be able to give public speeches, and Toastmasters was the obvious vehicle.

Angela's approach was profoundly different. As Chairperson and Board member for the Housing Co-op in which she lived, she was required to give monthly oral reports. In other words, she was a "public speaker" for twenty years before joining Toastmasters. Angela's neighbor asked her if she wanted to join Toastmasters. She had been to a meeting before as a guest. She thought, "Why not?! Maybe I'll meet some people there and make some friends." Of course, her Ice Breaker speech was magnificent. Now, even though she is fairly new, members look to her for tips and advice on speaking. She looks to them for the rules of how meetings should be run – the leadership track.

For Frederick, overcoming the initial fear of public speaking was troublesome after a lifetime of avoidance, but he was able to fall back on the discoveries he had made about himself in his own Life Purpose discovery process. Frederick's top values include having fun and achieving excellence. By knowing this about himself, he could focus on these values in his learning as a Toastmaster to guarantee success. In becoming determined to succeed at public speaking, Frederick used his Life Purpose statement to push himself – to make public speaking fun and to do it excellently. He created a mantra that he used after every disappointment: "I can do this, this will be fun! I can do this, this will be fun!" And before long, he could do it and it was fun! The later addition of Angela's teaching about gratitude, helped Frederick's speaking abilities by him realizing that every speech is a gift to the audience and a chance for gratitude for their attention and applause. This is the reason that Frederick's speeches are now so dynamic and entertaining and so much fun for himself and his audiences.

Angela recalls that when it came to doing Frederick's Life Purpose exercise, she found it quite easy to come up with her words and values. Why? Angela said, "It's because I have been through so many self-help programs, twelve step programs, women's therapy groups, etc., I had done similar work many times already. Frederick's approach to doing this Life Purpose exercise was intriguing to me. He had a way of putting a new spin on it, and it appealed to me immensely. Like the saying goes, 'When the student is ready, the teacher shall appear.' Frederick was my 'teacher' for the work I did on my Life Purpose."

While Frederick and Angela were working on this together in an online discussion forum, other members started joining in. Before long several people were discovering their own Life Purposes, and an interesting variety of Life Purposes and mission statements were being written.

Angela said, "I didn't need that much of a push to do the work, see the value of doing it, or that much help in 'tweaking' my Life Purpose. Others on the forum were having a tough time with it, though. Some of them forgot all about it and left it half finished. The difference for me, I think, was that I was ready to acknowledge that part of my soul that was screaming out to me – to allow myself to be a writer." Angela had always identified with being a broadcaster and voice-over artist. She had always identified with being a professional volunteer and victims' advocate. Now it was time to claim her identity as a writer, too.

Angela and Frederick are as different as night and day. Yet they each saw value in what the other had to teach. They saw value in taking the time to learn about and understand each other's point of view. A friendship began, although at first they had dismissed each other's views. It grew into curiosity over what the other meant, and led to a unique friendship and even becoming co-authors of this very book. Of course, there is a moral to the story—never be too quick to judge those you meet in real life or in cyberspace. As Angela says, "It's like the saying I have on my life purpose collage – 'Sometimes the best ideas sprout in the most unlikely places.' "

Frederick and Angela both live their lives proving to all around them that having a Life Purpose and living with gratitude and kindness are truly the foundations for a congruent and happy life – and that applies to business and friendships, too.

May you discover your true Life Purpose from doing this exercise, as we did. May you learn how to be grateful for everything you have in your life. And lastly, may you help spread the seeds for random acts of kindness wherever you go. You too may discover a unique friendship waiting for you. At the very least, we are sure you will find a great way to discover what your soul is longing to do. You will find the motivation within you to keep the desire to follow your dreams alive and well. You, too, can live the life of your dreams—living on purpose, with gratitude and kindness.

Best wishes,

Angela Christensen and Frederick Pearce – Authors.

"Life Purpose, gratitude, and kindness: they are the foundation of a congruent, happy life."

* * *

EPILOGUE

We hope, dear Reader, that you found all this information helpful! Congratulations for doing the work, too. And it was a lot of work, we admit. You just went through one heck of a whirlwind tour. We hope you found it fun. We feel as a boat builder might feel, having built the boat and now sending it forth on a voyage – with you the voyager on your life journey. As Frederick says in *his* Life Purpose statement: "I am a voyager: along the way I meet other travelers and add to their bounty however I can." We trust that we have added something to your bounty so you can build the life you want and deserve. We hope, too, that you will allow us the satisfaction of a job well done. Maybe soon, you will feel inclined to pass these lessons on to others – paying it forward.

Angela says, "My Life Purpose is to be a published author, thereby helping people through contribution, writing with love and integrity..." By granting us that, dear Reader, you have given us a great gift, and we are truly grateful. You have allowed us to share parts of our lives and skills with you. Our sincere hope is that what we have shared here has helped you find your Life Purpose and made you grateful for what you have and for what you will soon have even more – a harmonious and abundant life – an extraordinary life.

* * *

ABOUT THE AUTHORS

Angela Christensen is a forty-four year old freelance writer who lives in Calgary, Alberta, Canada. Angela has had many painful personal experiences and learned to overcome many obstacles in her life. Angela has a Broadcasting Degree and does voice-overs for commercials, documentaries and corporate videos. She is known for her smooth and pleasant voice.

Angela also has an extensive background in crime prevention and disaster relief work. She has had training by the Calgary Police Service, Vancouver Police Department and the Canadian Red Cross, as a volunteer – to mention but a few. Angela has been a Victims' Advocate for years, assisting those whose homes have been lost due to fire, helping victims of crime and helping the communities where she has lived. Angela has served on many boards and committees over the last twenty years. It is through her working on her own issues that she came to learn about gratitude, random acts of kindness and living her spirituality. Discovering her Life Purpose, she knew it was time to use her writing talents and experiences for the world at large.

Angela has a son, Matthew, who is in college and, like his mother, he wants to be a writer or editor, but only for the film industry. Angela also has two cats, Molly and Tatt. Angela's hobbies include stained glass, genealogy, hot air ballooning, arts and crafts and baking. Angela is currently working on four books of her own along with a screenplay about the issues which have affected her life. Angela is also a writer and contributor to many websites.

Frederick Pearce is sixty-five and retired, although he still performs some public speaking and business coaching. His thirty years of international experience as a Construction Specialist covers contracts, claims, planning and estimating/bidding. Frederick has been responsible for the financial management of construction projects, contractual management, and general management. This overlaps with many years of creating, planning, managing, guiding and consulting in small business, resulting in a successful and varied forty-five year career.

Frederick was born in England; lived in Germany, the Caribbean, Kuwait and other Gulf states. Since 1987 his home has been Houston, Texas. He has traveled to thirty-nine different countries and lived in seven of them, on four continents. In addition to his experience in the corporate world he has twenty-five years starting, developing, and growing various small businesses of his own.

As a Business Mentor. Frederick has learned to apply his work experience to the field of Personal Coaching. He works with business owners to develop personal and business strategies for company growth and improving personal life.

Frederick says he used to be very uptight and intense; now he is calmer and happier, having learned to be grateful! He won the *"rat race"* and retired. He has made mistakes and learned a lot of lessons, which he now shares with his clients. He was a workaholic, so understands what they are going through.

Both authors are good examples of the value of showing gratitude, carrying out random acts of kindness, and combining it all into a harmonious Life Purpose.

You can meet Angela and Frederick and other success-minded people at Successvibe—www.successvibe.com/forum

We look forward to seeing you there.

* * *

3154436

Made in the USA